TONY STEWART

IN THE FAST LANE

David and Patricia Armentrout

Rourke

Publishing LLC

Vero Beach, Florida 32964

www.rourkepublishing.com

PHOTO CREDITS: All photos ©Getty Images

Title page: *Tony Stewart makes a pit stop at Martinsville Speedway.*

Editor: Robert Stengard-Olliges

Cover design by Nicola Stratford

Library of Congress Cataloging-in-Publication Data

Armentrout, David, 1962-
  Tony Stewart : in the fast lane / David and Patricia Armentrout.
      p. cm. -- (In the fast lane)
  Includes index.
  ISBN 1-60044-221-8 (hardcover)
  ISBN 978-1-60044-314-5 (paperback)
  1. Stewart, Tony, 1971---Juvenile literature. 2. Stock car
drivers--United States--Biography--Juvenile literature. 3. NASCAR
(Association)--Juvenile literature. I. Armentrout, Patricia, 1960- II.
Title. III. Series.
  GV1032.S743A76 2007
  796.72092--dc22
                                        2006010685

Printed in the USA

CG/CG

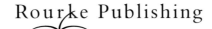

Rourke Publishing

www.rourkepublishing.com – sales@rourkepublishing.com
Post Office Box 3328, Vero Beach, FL 32964

TABLE OF CONTENTS

CHAMPION RACER

When it comes to racing, it's hard to find a more competitive and **versatile** driver than Tony Stewart. It doesn't matter if he's behind the wheel of a midget, a sprint, or a stock car; Tony's aggressive driving style keeps him in the fast lane.

Born: May 20, 1971
Organization: NASCAR
Car: Chevrolet #20
Car Owner: Joe Gibbs
Team: Joe Gibbs Racing
Sponsor: The Home Depot

Tony's success attracts the attention of NASCAR fans.

Tony's passion for racing began early in life. He started racing go-karts at the age of seven. In 1989, Tony began driving midgets and sprints cars. He performed well in all racing categories. In Fact, Tony won the Triple Crown—the National Midget, Sprint, and Silver Crown titles—in 1995. He was the first driver to win all three titles in the same year.

FAST FACTS

Midget, Sprint, Indy, and Formula One level racing are part of open wheel competition. Open wheel racecars have no fenders.

Tony is comfortable in just about any type of racecar. Here he gets ready to run a qualifying lap for the 1999 Indy 500.

INDY CAR EXCITEMENT

Racing an Indy car was Tony's big dream, so you can imagine how he felt when, in 1995, racing legend A. J. Foyt asked Tony to test drive his Indy car. Tony drove so well that Foyt offered him three races in the 1996 **inaugural** season of the Indy Racing League (**IRL**). Tony had already agreed to drive a stock car in NASCAR's Busch **series**, so he decided to turn down Foyt's offer.

*Former driver and Indy
car owner A. J. Foyt.*

Tony then test drove an Indy car for John Menard and landed a spot on the Menard Indy car team. He raced three open wheel races in 1996 and was voted **Rookie** of the Year. Tony also raced nine **NASCAR** Busch Series events and one Craftsman Truck race. Tony got plenty of practice in '96 racing any kind of car he could.

Tony gets pushed out of the pit at the 1997 Indy 500.

DOUBLE DUTY

Tony joined NASCAR's Joe Gibbs Racing team in 1997, and continued to race for Menard in the IRL. Tony won his first IRL race that year and ended the season as the IRL champion. In 1998, Tony finished third in the IRL, and raced in 22 Busch events.

Racing in both IRL and NASCAR events became more and more difficult to schedule. Tony knew he had to make a choice. He would continue to race in select IRL events, but would focus most of his time on stock car racing.

Tony finished third in this 1997 Busch race driving the #44 Shell Pontiac.

Tony first competed in the Winston Cup series (now Nextel Cup), the top level in NASCAR, in 1999. In 34 starts, Tony had 21 top-ten finishes and three wins. It's no surprise he was named Rookie of the Year.

Tony was also the first driver to finish the Indy 500 and NASCAR's Coca-Cola 600 in the same day! He pulled it off again in 2001. By then, Tony was well known for his "Double Duty" racing.

Tony climbs into his racecar prior to the 85th running of the Indy 500 in 2001.

FAST FACTS

NASCAR Point System for Each Race

Winner   driver earns 180 points

Runner-up   driver earns 170 points

3rd-6th position   points drop in 5-point increments
(3rd position-165 points, 4th-160, 5th-155, and 6th-150 points)

7th-11th position   points drop in 4-point increments

12th-42nd position points drop in 3-point increments

Last place   driver earns 34 points

**Drivers can earn bonus points for leading
a lap and leading the most laps**

Tony celebrates his 2002 Cup championship.

BAD START, GREAT FINISH

The Daytona 500 is NASCAR's first and biggest event of the season, but the 2002 race didn't last long for Tony. His engine blew up after the second lap and he finished last.

FAST FACTS

NASCAR began its 2004 season with a new Cup sponsor—Nextel Communications. NASCAR also began a new system for crowning the Cup champion, called 'NASCAR's Chase for the Nextel Cup.' The Chase consists of the final ten races of the 36-race schedule. The top ten drivers in the point standings from the first 26 races, and any driver within 400 points of the leader, are eligible for the prize.

Tony managed to turn things around, though. By the end of the season, Tony placed in the top five 15 times, and racked up enough points to win the Winston Cup **championship**—the organization's greatest prize.

Jamie McMurray and Tony Stewart lead as racers take a turn at Talladega.

THE BUSINESS OF RACING

Tony's success in racing has brought him celebrity status and a lot of money. But the reason Tony races is because he enjoys competition and he loves to win.

When Tony is not racing in NASCAR, or running his own motorsports business, he's on the track in a sprint or midget car. Tony also owns a sprint car driven by Danny Lasoski in the World of Outlaws racing series.

Tony and team celebrate his second Cup championship in 2005.

CHASING THE CUP

Winning the 2002 championship was huge for Tony, but that accomplishment didn't give Tony a license to slow down. Tony won two races in 2003 and again in 2004. Tony's 2005 season was even better. He won five Nextel Cup races and finished the season on top, winning his second Cup championship.

Career Highlights

2005: NASCAR Nextel Cup champion

2004: Won two Nextel Cup races and finished sixth in points

2003: Won two Winston Cup races and finished seventh in points

2002: NASCAR Winston Cup champion

2001: Won three Winston Cup races and finished second in points

2000: Won six Winston Cup races and finished sixth in points

1999: Named Winston Cup series Rookie of the Year

1998: First to complete the Indy 500 and the Coca-Cola 600 in the same day, driving more racing miles in one day than any other driver!

1997: Indy Racing League champion

GLOSSARY

championship (CHAM pee uhn ship) — each driver is awarded points in a race, with winners earning the most. The driver with the most points at the end of a season wins the championship

inaugural (in AWG eh rel) — marking a beginning

IRL — Indy Racing League: a promoter of open-wheel racing in 1996

NASCAR — National Association for Stock Car Auto Racing: the governing body for the Nextel Cup, Craftsman Truck, and Busch series, among others

rookie (ROOK ee) — a first-year driver

series (SIHR eez) — a group of races that make up one season

versatile (VER set uhl) — moving from one thing to another with ease

INDEX

FURTHER READING

Stewart, Tony. *True Speed: My Racing Life*. Harper Entertainment, 2002.
Teitelbaum, Michael. *Tony Stewart, Instant Superstar*. Tradition Books, 2002.
White, Ben. *NASCAR Racers: Today's Top Drivers*. Motorbooks International, 2003.

WEBSITES TO VISIT

www.nascar.com
www.homedepotracing.com
www.joegibbsracing.com
www.racingone.com

ABOUT THE AUTHORS

David and Patricia Armentrout have written many nonfiction books for young readers. They have had several books published for primary school reading. The Armentrouts live in Cincinnati, Ohio, with their two children.